On the Road

The Porsche 911

by Michael Burgan

Consultant:
Bruce Anderson
Technical Chairman
Porsche Club of America

RiverFront Books

an imprint of Franklin Watts
A Division of Grolier Publishing
New York   London   Hong Kong   Sydney
Danbury, Connecticut

RiverFront Books
http://publishing.grolier.com

Library of Congress Cataloging-in-Publication Data
Burgan, Michael.
    The Porsche 911/by Michael Burgan.
    p. cm.—(On the road)
    Includes bibliographical references (p. 44) and index.
    Summary: Describes the history, development, and design of the various
models of Porsche 911s that have been made since its introduction in 1964.
    ISBN 0-7368-0183-9
    1. Porsche 911 automobile—History—Juvenile literature.
[1. Porsche 911 automobile.] I. Title. II. Series: On the road (Mankato, Minn.)
TL215.P75B87 1999
629.222'2—dc21   98-48708
                                                             CIP
                                                             AC

Editorial Credits
Blake Hoena, editor; Timothy Halldin, cover designer; Linda Clavel, illustrator;
    Sheri Gosewisch and Kimberly Danger, photo researchers

Photo Credits
Bob Schneider, 22
Corbis-Bettmann/UPI, 7; Corbis/The National Archives, 10, 12
Photri-Microstock/Novak, cover
The Picture Cube/Walter Bibikow, 15; Jerry Austin, 23
Ronald Cantor, 20, 21, 45
Ron Kimball, 16, 24, 25, 26, 29, 31, 37
Unicorn Stock Photos/V. E. Horne, 32–33
Uniphoto 4; Uniphoto/Allan Laidman, 9
Visuals Unlimited/Jeff Greenberg, 18, 41

Table of Contents

Chapter 1

Porsche Cars

The Porsche 911 is a sports car. A sports car is designed for performance. A car's performance includes speed and handling. The 1999 Porsche 911 has a top speed of 174 miles (280 kilometers) per hour. The Porsche 911 also handles well. A driver can steer this car easily at high speeds.

Cars made by the Porsche company are known for quality. Engineers build their engines by hand. These engines then are tested before being used. This assures the engines work properly. Porsche automobiles also are reliable. They do not break down often. About 70 percent of all Porsches ever made are still being driven today.

Many old Porsches are still being driven today.

The Founder of Porsche

In 1875, Ferdinand Porsche was born in Bohemia. Bohemia is now part of the Czech Republic in Eastern Europe. Ferdinand had a talent for working with electricity. He set up an electrical system for lighting in his parents' house at age 18. A company that made electrical equipment and machines hired Ferdinand that same year.

In 1898, Jacob Lohner & Company hired Ferdinand. This company made horse-drawn coaches. But the company's owner thought electric cars would replace coaches. Ferdinand designed his first car in 1900 for this company. The car was called the Lohner-Porsche Chaise.

Ferdinand was interested in racing the cars he built. The Lohner-Porsche Chaise set a speed record on the Semmering Road. This road was a 6-mile (10-kilometer) course near Vienna, Austria. The Lohner-Porsche Chaise traveled this road in 14 minutes and 53 seconds.

In 1924, Ferdinand designed a car that won the Targa Florio race. The Targa Florio is

Ferdinand Porsche designed many winning race cars.

a race driven on the roads of Sicily. The car Ferdinand designed was a Mercedes Benz. He built it for Dailmer Motors AG in Stuttgart, Germany.

In 1930, Ferdinand started his own car design company. This company also built many successful race cars. In 1970, a Porsche race car won the 24 Hours of Le Mans for the first time. This race is held in France each year. In this race, teams of drivers race around a track for 24 hours. The drivers in a team can only stop their car for gasoline, repairs, or to switch drivers. A Porsche automobile has won the Le Mans 16 times between 1970 and 1998.

The Porsche 911

The Porsche 911 is one of the Porsche company's most popular cars. In 1998, the Porsche company began selling a new model of this car. The company spent more than $500 million to design the new Porsche 911. This model is longer than earlier Porsche 911 models. It also has a more powerful engine. But the Porsche company did not change the

The Porsche 911 handles well at high speeds.

car's most popular features. The Porsche 911 is still a fast car that handles well.

New Porsche 911s cost about $70,000. Some sports cars handle better or are faster than Porsche 911s. But these other sports cars can cost hundreds of thousands of dollars. Many car experts believe Porsche 911s are the best sports cars in their price range.

Chapter 2

Porsche's Beginnings

Ferdinand Porsche started his own auto design company in 1930. He called his company the Porsche Bureau. The first car his company designed was for the Wanderer Firm in Chemnitz, Germany. This car was called the Wanderer. It became popular in Germany.

In 1934, Adolf Hitler was the leader of Germany. He wanted a cheap and reliable car for the German people. Hitler hired Ferdinand to design this car. Hitler named this car Volkswagen. Volkswagen means "people's car" in German. Ferdinand's design was later called the Beetle. It had a rounded back and people thought it looked like a bug. The Beetle became very popular. More than 21 million Beetles have been sold. It is the world's best-selling car.

More Beetles have been produced than any other model of car.

Porsche's First Sports Car

In 1948, Ferdinand and his son Ferry Porsche completed the design of the Porsche 356. This was the first automobile the Porsche company designed that was given the family name. The Porsche 356 had a top speed of 85 miles (137 kilometers) per hour. Its engine was in the rear of the car. The first Porsche 356 had room for the driver and one passenger. It did not have a roof.

Later models of the Porsche 356 held up to four passengers and had a hard roof. A sports car with a hard roof is called a coupe.

Sports car enthusiasts liked how the Porsche 356 performed. The Porsche company started to receive orders for the Porsche 356. But the company was small and had few employees. It could make only five cars per month. In 1950, the company expanded and could make up to 10 cars per month.

Family Tradition

Designing cars became a Porsche family tradition. Ferry's son also was interested in building cars. His name was Ferdinand

All Porsche engines are built by hand.

Alexander "Butzi" Porsche. In 1959, Butzi began designing the Porsche 901. In 1964, the Porsche company began selling this car and changed its name to the Porsche 911.

The Porsche 911 is a coupe. It also was sold as a "2 plus 2" automobile. This means it has two front seats and two back seats. But the back seats are only big enough for children or to hold luggage.

The Porsche 911 had a bigger engine than the Porsche 356. The Porsche 911 had a six-cylinder engine. The Porsche 356 engine had only four cylinders. Cylinders are hollow metal tubes in an engine where gasoline is burned.

Porsche 911 engines had two things in common with Porsche 356 engines. Both types of engines were in the rear of the cars. Both engines also were cooled by air. Many car engines are cooled by water that flows through tubes. But air-cooled engines use air from outside the car to cool the engine parts. Air also helps engines burn gasoline. Air-cooled engines burn gasoline more completely than water-cooled engines.

The Porsche 356 had an air-cooled engine with four cylinders.

Chapter 3

Porsche 911 Models

The Porsche company made and sold 232 Porsche 911s in 1964. It produced about 10,000 Porsche 911s in 1965. In 1966, the Porsche company made its 100,000th car.

The Porsche 911 continued the winning tradition of Porsche-built race cars. In 1965, a Porsche 911 won the Monte Carlo Rally. This race starts in Monte Carlo, Monaco, and continues through the mountains of southern France. In 1967, another Porsche 911 set a speed record at the Monza track in Italy. This car was driven 12,430 miles (20,004 kilometers) in 95 hours. The car's average speed was 130 miles (209 kilometers) per hour.

The Porsche company has built many successful race cars.

The Porsche 911S had a more powerful engine than the standard Porsche 911.

New Models

In 1967, the Porsche company sold the Targa model of the Porsche 911. The Targa was named after the Targa Florio race in Sicily. The Targa was called a safety convertible. The car's roof was removable and its rear window folded down. The Targa also had a roll bar behind the driver and front passenger's seat. A roll bar protects the driver and passengers if a car flips over.

In 1967, the Porsche company sold the Porsche 911S. This car had a more powerful engine than the standard Porsche 911. The standard Porsche 911 had an engine that produced 130 horsepower. Horsepower is a measure of an engine's power. The Porsche 911S engine produced 160 horsepower.

More Power and Better Handling

In 1970, the Porsche company put a larger, more powerful engine in all Porsche 911 models. The size of this engine was nearly 134 cubic inches (2,195 cubic centimeters). Engine size is the measure of the space inside the engine's cylinders where gasoline is burned. The Porsche 911S engine then produced 180 horsepower.

In 1972, the Porsche company again increased the engine size in all Porsche 911 models. This engine was nearly 143 cubic inches (2,341 cubic centimeters). It produced 190 horsepower in the Porsche 911S.

The Porsche company made other changes to the Porsche 911. These changes improved the car's handling. The Porsche company added

Air dams below a car's bumper help prevent wind from getting under the car.

wider tires to the Porsche 911. They also added air dams. These flaps are below the front bumpers on cars. They help keep wind from getting under cars. This makes cars easier to steer at high speeds.

The Carrera

In 1972, the Porsche company built the Carrera RS model of the Porsche 911. Porsche named this car after the Carrera Pan-American race held in Mexico. The Carrera engine was nearly

164 cubic inches (2,687 cubic centimeters). This engine produced 210 horsepower and had a top speed of 149 miles (240 kilometers) per hour.

Carreras had air dams to improve their handling at high speeds. They also had spoilers. A spoiler is a stiff flap across the back of some cars. Air flowing over a car's spoiler pushes down on the car's back end. This improves a car's handling at high speeds. The spoiler on the Carrera looked like a duck's tail. This style of spoiler became known as a rear duck-tail spoiler.

A spoiler improves a car's handling at high speeds.

The Turbo 911 Porsche

In 1975, the Porsche company designed a new engine for the Porsche 911. This engine had a turbocharger. A turbocharger forces more air into the engine's cylinders than a standard engine. This extra air helps the engine burn gasoline more quickly. This produces more power. The engine in the Porsche 911 Turbo produced 260 horsepower.

The Porsche 911 Turbo's engine forces extra air into the engine to produce more power.

A convertible has a cloth roof that folds back.

Porsche 911 Turbos had many special features. These features included leather seats, air conditioning, and headlight washers. But most people bought Porsche 911 Turbos for their speed. Porsche 911 Turbos reached a speed of 160 miles (257 kilometers) per hour.

Other Models

In 1982, the Porsche company began selling a Porsche 911 convertible. This car had a cloth

The Porsche 911 Twin Turbo was the most powerful car the Porsche company mass produced.

roof that folded back. The Porsche 911 convertible was called a Cabriolet. Some people called it a Cabrio for short.

The Carrera 4 was another model of the Porsche 911. This model was first sold in 1989. The Carrera 4 had four-wheel drive. Power from the engine turns all four wheels of a four-wheel-drive vehicle. This made the Carrera 4 easier to drive on snowy or muddy roads.

In 1995, the Porsche company mass produced its most powerful car. This car was the Porsche 911 Twin Turbo. Its engine produced 400 horsepower.

In 1996, the Porsche company built a racing model of the Porsche 911. This car was called the GT1. The Porsche GT1 was the first Porsche 911 to have its engine in the front of the car. All earlier Porsche 911s had their engines in the rear.

The GT1 was a racing model of the Porsche 911.

Chapter 4

The New Porsche

In 1998, the Porsche company began to sell a new Porsche 911 Carrera in North America. This is the 1999 model of the Porsche 911. The 1999 model can be ordered as either a coupe or a convertible.

A New Body
The Porsche company made the 1999 Porsche 911 slightly larger than older Porsche 911 models. It is more than 14 feet (443 centimeters) long and almost 6 feet (177 centimeters) wide. But the 1999 Porsche 911 weighs less than older models. The Porsche company used lighter metals to build the 1999 Porsche 911. One of these metals is aluminum.

The Targa model of the Porsche 911 was named after the Targa Florio race in Sicily.

Aluminum is lighter than steel. But it is very strong. Boron is another lightweight metal used in the 1999 Porsche 911. Boron is a very strong type of steel. Boron adds strength to the 1999 Porsche 911 body.

The 1999 Porsche 911 also looks different than older models. Its fenders are closer to the car's body than the fenders of older models. The front windshield is closer to the passengers. This style of windshield and a new roof design give drivers and passengers more headroom.

The 1999 Porsche 911 has a spoiler in the rear. But the spoiler is not visible until the car reaches a speed of 75 miles (121 kilometers) per hour. The spoiler then raises to help improve the car's handling at high speeds.

Safety Features

The Porsche company is the first German automaker to put air bags in all of its cars. Air bags inflate when a vehicle crashes. They help protect the driver and front-seat passenger. One air bag is located in the steering wheel. Another is located in the vehicle's dashboard in front of the front passenger's seat.

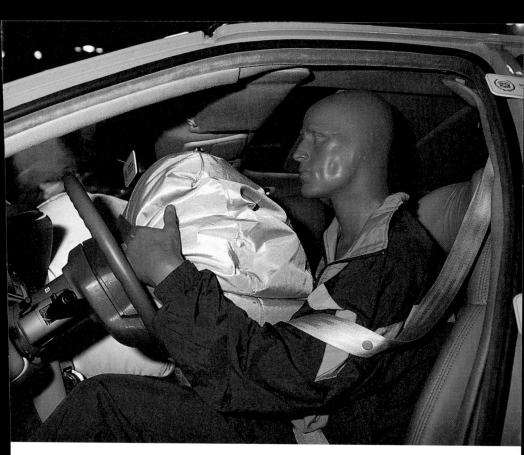

Air bags inflate like balloons to protect the driver and front-seat passenger.

The 1999 Porsche 911 has other safety features. Side air bags inflate if a car is hit on the side. The car's doors also have boron steel beams inside them. These beams and air bags reduce the chance of injuries from side collisions.

The 1999 Porsche 911 convertible has an additional safety feature. This car has two roll bars hidden behind the back seats. A computer in the 1999 Porsche 911 senses if the car is about to flip over. These roll bars then raise to protect the drivers and passengers.

A New Engine

The Porsche company made changes to the engine in the 1999 Porsche 911. This was the first Porsche 911 to have a water-cooled engine. The Porsche company believed this water-cooled engine would be cleaner and more powerful than an air-cooled engine.

The 1999 Porsche 911 engine is nearly 207 cubic inches (3,387 cubic centimeters). This engine produces 296 horsepower. The 1999 Porsche 911 has a top speed of 174 miles (280 kilometers) per hour.

Tradition is important to Porsche owners. Some owners did not want the design of the Porsche 911 to change. Some Porsche owners were disappointed that the 1999 Porsche 911 engine is not air cooled. But the Porsche company assured owners this new engine is the best it has ever built. The Porsche company also told owners that all engines are still built by hand and tested. This assures their quality.

The Porsche company uses a water-cooled engine in the 1999 Porsche 911.

1972 Porsche 911

Parts of an Engine

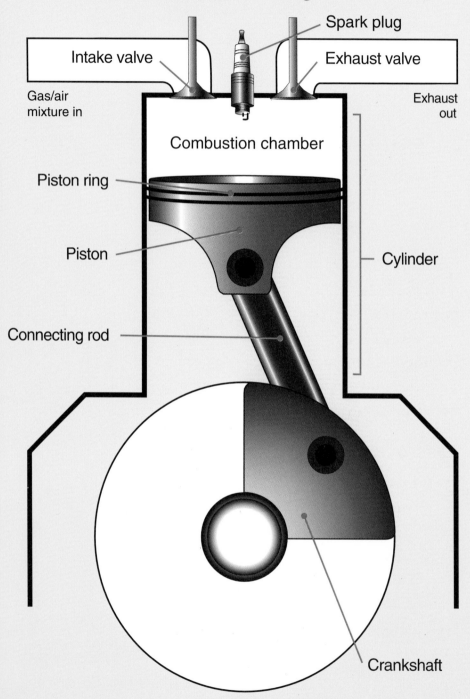

Intake valve

Spark plug

Exhaust valve

Gas/air
mixture in

Exhaust
out

Combustion chamber

Piston ring

Piston

Cylinder

Connecting rod

Crankshaft

Quick Facts about Engines

Most cars and trucks have internal combustion engines. Internal combustion creates power by burning gasoline inside engines. This power turns the wheels of vehicles. Internal combustion engines also are used in motorcycles and lawn mowers.

Parts of an Internal Combustion Engine

Cylinder: The cylinder is a hollow metal tube in the engine. A lawn mower has one cylinder. Most cars and trucks have four, six, or eight cylinders.

Internal combustion engines are used in most cars, trucks, motorcycles, and lawn mowers.

Combustion chamber: The combustion chamber is the space inside the cylinder. A gasoline and air mixture is burned in the combustion chamber.

Intake valve: Gasoline and air enter the combustion chamber through a hole in the top of the cylinder. The intake valve opens and closes this hole. A cylinder usually has one intake valve.

Exhaust valve: Exhaust leaves the combustion chamber through a hole in the top of the cylinder. The exhaust valve opens and closes this hole. A cylinder usually has one exhaust valve.

Spark plugs: Spark plugs light the gasoline and air mixture in the combustion chamber. This makes the gasoline burn.

Piston: The piston is a round piece of metal that moves up and down in the cylinder.

Piston rings: Piston rings stop air, gasoline, and exhaust from leaking out of the combustion chamber.

Most Porsche engines are in the rear of the car.

Crankshaft: The up-and-down motion of the piston turns the crankshaft. This spinning motion applies power to the wheels of a vehicle.

Connecting rod: The connecting rod connects the piston to the crankshaft.

The Engine Cycle

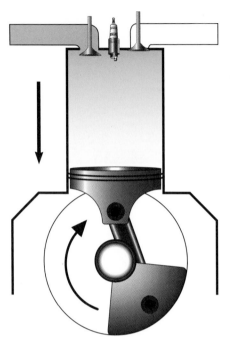

1. Intake

The piston moves down and the intake valve opens. Air and gasoline enter the combustion chamber.

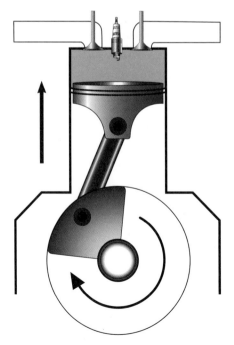

2. Compression

The intake valve closes. The piston then moves up. This upward movement forces the air and gasoline into a smaller space. This action is called compression. Compression also pushes the mixture of air and gasoline into contact with the spark plug.

3. Combustion

The spark plug lights the air and gasoline mixture. The burning mixture pushes the piston down.

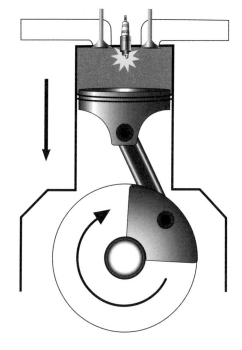

4. Exhaust

The exhaust valve opens. The piston moves up. This pushes burned gasoline out of the combustion chamber.

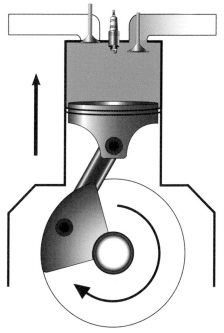

The four stages in the engine cycle are intake, compression, combustion, and exhaust.

The Power of an Engine

Engines create power by burning gasoline. Engines that burn more gasoline in each cycle create more power. People can do two things to make engines burn more gasoline. They can add more cylinders to engines. They also can make the cylinders larger.

Horsepower is a measurement of an engine's power. One horsepower is the force needed to move 33,000 pounds (14,969 kilograms) a distance of 12 inches (30 centimeters) in one minute.

Cars with more powerful engines often can reach faster speeds. The 1972 Porsche 911 Carrera had nearly a 164-cubic-inch (2,687-cubic-centimeter) engine. This engine produced 210 horsepower. This car had a top speed of 149 miles (240 kilometers) per hour. The 1999 Porsche 911 Carrera's engine is nearly 207 cubic inches (3,387 cubic centimeters). This engine produces 296 horsepower. This car has a top speed of 174 miles (280 kilometers) per hour.

Cars with larger, more powerful engines often can reach faster speeds.

Words to Know

air bags (AIR BAGSS)—safety features that inflate like balloons when a car crashes; air bags protect the driver and front-seat passenger in a crash.

air-cooled engine (AIR-KOOLD EN-juhn)—an engine that uses air from outside the engine to cool its parts

air dams (AIR DAMSS)—flaps below a car's bumper that prevent wind from getting under the car

convertible (kuhn-VUR-tuh-buhl)—a car with a cloth top that folds back

coupe (KOOP)—a sports car with a hard roof

four-wheel drive (FOR-WEEL DRIVE)—a drive system that allows power from an engine to turn all four wheels of a vehicle at the same time

horsepower (HORSS-pou-ur)—the measure of an engine's power

internal combustion engine (in-TUR-nuhl kuhm-BUSS-chuhn EN-juhn)—an engine that creates power by burning gasoline inside

performance (pur-FOR-muhnss)—combination of a sports car's speed and handling

roll bar (ROHL BAR)—a bar located behind the driver and front-seat passenger; the roll bar helps prevent injuries if a car flips over.

spoiler (SPOIL-ur)—a stiff flap across the back of a car; a spoiler improves a car's handling at high speeds.

sports car (SPORTSS KAR)—a car designed for its speed and handling

turbocharger (TUR-boh-charj-ur)—an engine system that forces extra air into an engine

water-cooled engine (WAW-tur-KOOLD EN-juhn)—an engine that has water flowing through tubes to keep its parts cool

To Learn More

Adler, Dennis. *Porsche 911 Road Cars*. Osceola, Wis.: MBI Publishing, 1998.

Italia, Rob. *Great Auto Makers and Their Cars*. Minneapolis: The Oliver Press, 1993.

Jay, Jackson. *Super Sports Cars*. Mankato, Minn.: Capstone Press, 1996.

Lally, Linda. *The Volkswagen Beetle*. On the Road. Mankato, Minn.: Capstone Press, 1999.

Schleifer, Jay. *Porsche: Germany's Wonder Car*. New York: Crestwood House, 1992.

Useful Addresses

Porsche Cars North America
980 Hammond Drive, Suite 1000
Atlanta, GA 30328

Porsche Club of America
P.O. Box 30100
Alexandria, VA 22310-8100

Porsche Club of America/Canada West Region
385 Monteray Avenue
North Vancouver, BC V7N 3E7
Canada

Sports Car Club of America
9033 East Easter Place
Englewood, CO 80112

Internet Sites

Porsche Club of America
http://www.pca.org

Porsche Club of America/Upper Canada Region
http://www.pca.org/ucr

Porsche Net
http://www.porsche-net.com

Porsche Cars North America
http://porsche.genex.com/home.html

Index